Why this book?

- Do you, or does a loved one, suffer from diabetes?
- Have you been recently diagnosed and want to know more?
- Are you bewildered by all the information out there?

Diabetes is a common condition, which can be fatal. It needs careful managing, and for that you need clear and accurate information – written in a way you can understand.
This book explains

- what diabetes is – both Types 1 and 2
- how it affects your body
- what you need to do to manage it properly
- the implications of badly managed diabetes.

Many people learn to live with their diabetes and have good health. Armed with the right information, you can control your diabetes – rather than it controlling you.

For Nikki, Harry, Sam, and Archie
with lots of love

First Steps
to living with
Diabetes

Dr Simon Atkins

LION

Text copyright © 2016 Simon Atkins
This edition copyright © 2016 Lion Hudson

Published by Lion Books
an imprint of
Lion Hudson plc
Wilkinson House, Jordan Hill Road,
Oxford OX2 8DR, England
www.lionhudson.com/lion

ISBN 978 0 7459 7043 1
e-ISBN 978 0 7459 7044 8

First edition 2016

Acknowledgments
Drawings pp. 22, 89, 90 © Sam Atkins

A catalogue record for this book is available from the British Library

Printed and bound in the UK, January 2016, LH26

Contents

Introduction

There's an episode of the classic BBC television series *Only Fools and Horses* in which Derek "Del Boy" Trotter jokes that his brother Rodney's work colleague Elvis is so daft that he thinks Sugar Diabetes is a Welsh flyweight boxer. Although we might laugh along with Del at the lad's ignorance, many of us will feel some sympathy for him – because young Elvis is in very good company when it comes to being confused about diabetes.

As misunderstood diseases go, diabetes is right up there at the top of the list alongside some of the rarest medical conditions, despite the fact that it is anything but rare itself. Statistics tell us that it affects around 3.2 million people in the UK and 29 million in the United States; globally, the World Health Organization estimates that a whopping 9 per cent of adults have diabetes. Given those numbers, we are all likely to have first-hand knowledge of someone who has it.

Even if you don't, it's not as if it's been kept secret. It's in the news almost every week, either because of a fresh government plan to combat it, or because of a spurious front-page splash in one of the tabloids linking it to everything from drinking coffee to taking antibiotics.

Despite the statistics and media coverage, however, many of us remain as confused about its true nature as Rodney's mate Elvis, with myths about the disease being so widespread that they are often believed to be facts.

The aim of this book, then, is to make things clearer, not only by debunking the myths, which you'll find along the way as you read through the book, but by explaining the facts as plainly and simply as possible.

We will look at what diabetes actually is and discuss the two main types of the condition (imaginatively called Type 1 and Type 2), highlighting their differences, similarities, and probable causes. There is also a chapter about the way in which it can affect particular groups of people such as children, pregnant women, and older adults.

The following chapters also run through the different treatments available and suggestions for lifestyle changes – diet, exercise, and stopping smoking – that can help minimize the chances of developing some of diabetes' more severe complications. Because, as we'll see, if uncontrolled and left to its own devices, diabetes can have devastating consequences, from heart disease and stroke to limb amputation.

But the good news is that it doesn't have to end up like that. The latest treatments can be extremely effective in controlling blood sugar, and by accessing the right support, eating an appropriate diet, and following a regular exercise routine, life can still be lived very much to the full.

1

What is diabetes?

Diabetes mellitus – to give it its full name – is a common, lifelong medical condition in which people have abnormally high levels of blood sugar. If it's not controlled, it affects many of the body's vital organs because of the damage it causes to nerves and blood vessels.

It is a disease that has an impact on the body's metabolism by affecting the control of levels of sugar in the blood. If you'd like to know more about the nitty-gritty of the science behind the condition, then head for Appendix 1, where you'll find a bit more about the biology of the hormone insulin and how, when its mechanisms become faulty, people can develop diabetes.

Diabetes by numbers

British diabetes charities reckon that there are currently 3 million people in the UK with one of the two types of diabetes. And the International Diabetes Federation reports that it affects around 387 million people worldwide, with the following distribution across the different regions of the globe:

Western Pacific, including Australia and New Zealand	South East Asia	Europe	North America and the Caribbean	The Middle East and North Africa	South and Central America	Sub-Saharan Africa
138 million	75 million	52 million	39 million	37 million	25 million	22 million

Figures from the International Diabetes Federation Report 2014 (www.idf.org)

They also estimate that a whopping 46 per cent of cases of diabetes are still undiagnosed and by 2035 there will be another 205 million people around the world who have the diagnosis.

Many in the "undiagnosed" group have what is known as pre-diabetes; the remainder already have either the Type 1 or Type 2 form of diabetes itself and just don't know it yet.

Pre-diabetes

Pre-diabetes is also called borderline diabetes because people with this have higher than normal levels of blood sugar but the readings don't yet meet the criteria for full-on diabetes. People in this category are thought to be likely to go on to develop Type 2 diabetes (see below) over the following ten years.

This is by no means a foregone conclusion, though, and research so far suggests that only 50 per cent of people with pre-diabetes will go on to develop diabetes. As a result, there is some controversy about this "diagnosis" among medical experts around the world.

In the USA, for example, there are very definite criteria for its diagnosis (see table in Chapter 4), with those fitting the bill having intensive input from health professionals who not only encourage lifestyle improvements but may also prescribe the drug metformin which, as we'll see in Chapter 8, is only used in the UK to treat definite diabetes. In fact, in the UK there are no agreed blood results for diagnosis of pre-diabetes and it is not recognized as an official diagnosis by the World Health Organization.

However, most doctors and nurses will advise people who fit the American criteria about lifestyle changes they could make to reduce their risk of developing Type 2 diabetes.

Type 1 diabetes

This is the less common variety of the disease, which affects around 1 in 300 people in the UK, accounting for around 10 per cent of all cases of diabetes. It typically arises in children and young adults, hence its previous names of childhood or juvenile diabetes and early-onset diabetes, and it is rare (although not impossible) to see a new diagnosis in people over the age of 40.

In this type of diabetes the pancreas stops making insulin and so there is a loss of control of blood sugar levels. Type 1 diabetes is therefore treated by making up for the body's lack of this hormone with regular injections of insulin. This gives it another of its previous names: insulin-dependent diabetes.

It's thought that Type 1 diabetes is an autoimmune disease in which a person's immune system attacks part of their own body. This happens in a number of other well-known medical conditions such as rheumatoid arthritis. In Type 1 diabetes the immune system attacks the pancreas gland, with the direct result that it stops making insulin. It's believed that this immune attack can be triggered by a virus infection.

Type 1 diabetes can run in families and the risk of developing it increases if your parents or siblings have the condition. And the more close relatives who have it, the higher the risk.

Type 2 diabetes

This is by far the most common form of diabetes, accounting for 90 per cent of cases and therefore equating to around 337.5 million people worldwide at current levels of diagnosis. It's a disease that historically only affected people over the age of 40 (it used to be called adult-onset diabetes) but it's now also being seen in young people and even children.

This is because, unlike Type 1 diabetes, which we've seen is an autoimmune disease, Type 2 diabetes is largely caused by obesity. We're currently in the grip of an obesity epidemic affecting men, women, and children across the developed world. In fact, the World Health Organization estimated in 2014 that there were 1.9 billion overweight adults globally (39 per cent of the world's adult population), with 6 million (13 per cent of adults) being obese.

The figures for children show that a staggering 42 million under-fives around the planet are either overweight or obese. It's no wonder, then, that the number of people developing Type 2 diabetes is predicted to rise dramatically over the next 20 years.

There are two reasons why people develop Type 2 diabetes:

- reduced production of insulin
- insulin resistance, where cells become less responsive to the effects of the insulin that is produced.

It is treated with a combination of lifestyle advice, particularly aimed at helping people to lose weight, and medication. It used to be called non-insulin-dependent diabetes because insulin injections were very rarely used in treatment, but that is no longer the case. If pills and lifestyle changes don't keep sugar levels under control in Type 2, then insulin may well be needed.

What is obesity?

The definition of obesity is based on a person's Body Mass Index (BMI), which is calculated from their height and weight measurements. It works for everyone, regardless of age and sex.

The calculation involves dividing a person's weight in kilogrammes by the square of their height in metres. The World Health Organization uses the following levels for its definitions:
- BMI greater than or equal to 25 means you are **overweight**.
- BMI greater than or equal to 30 means you are **obese**.

Mythbuster

Diabetes isn't really that serious.
Unfortunately, that couldn't be further from the truth. Diabetes comes eighth in the World Health Organization's list of Top Ten causes of death and it increases the risk of developing the top two on the list: heart disease and stroke.

2

What are the symptoms?

Spotting the symptoms of diabetes, be it Type 1 or Type 2, is crucial, as it means that treatment can be started as early as possible and the risks of developing the complications considered in Chapter 9 will be greatly reduced. Although there are many overlaps in the sets of symptoms produced by both types of diabetes, they each have some of their own unique features too. In this chapter we will look at both.

These symptoms will also depend on whether your body has too much or too little sugar whizzing around in the bloodstream at any one time. Even after diabetes is diagnosed, it's important to be aware of the warning signs for both situations.

We will also look at the symptoms of diabetic ketoacidosis, a potentially life-threatening medical emergency.

Before diagnosis

The most common symptoms of diabetes are the same regardless of which type of the condition is triggering them. They are caused by the effects of high levels of sugar in the bloodstream and the loss of the usual mechanisms for allowing it to be taken up into cells to be used as energy.

In Type 1 diabetes, the symptoms present suddenly and most often in children and younger people. In Type 2, however, the onset tends to be much more gradual, occurring in adults who will generally, but not always, be on the obese end of the weight spectrum. The main early symptoms are:

- *Polydipsia*. This is the technical term for a severe and persistent thirst despite drinking decent volumes of fluid during the day. It can be accompanied by an ongoing feeling of having a dry mouth, which is not relieved by drinking more. It occurs when the level of glucose in the blood becomes too high for it to be reabsorbed in the kidneys and so it is passed out in urine, taking more water with it than would usually be passed. This causes dehydration and thirst, and is the cause of the next symptom below.

- *Polyuria*. This describes the need to pass abnormally large volumes of urine very frequently every day. Polyuria is diagnosed when people find themselves peeing out more than three litres of urine in a 24-hour period; a more usual output would range from one to two litres. It will invariably go hand in hand with polydipsia.

- *Polyphagia*. This is the term used to describe an increased appetite, which will usually accompany the other two symptoms above. This increase will be felt as a desire to eat more food, more often.

- *Fatigue*. The experience of feeling tired all the time (or TATT as we abbreviate it in the trade) is one of the most common reasons for people to visit their family doctor. It can have many causes, including anaemia, abnormal thyroid gland function, stress and depression, heavy drug and alcohol use, a busy non-stop life due to burning the candle at both ends or perhaps the recent arrival of a baby in the family, and, not surprisingly, persistent lack of sleep. It can also be triggered by diabetes, because cells are being starved of their main energy supply, glucose. One of the tests doctors will run when people are TATT is a check of blood glucose levels, especially if accompanied by the other symptoms listed above.

- *Unexplained weight loss.* Losing weight without dieting is another of those worrying problems that people consult family doctors about, which can have many underlying causes. Cancer is one potential trigger that, not surprisingly, most people are concerned about when they start to drop waist and dress sizes without trying. It is not the most common reason, though, and others include thyroid gland problems, depression, dementia, smoking, use of recreational drugs, infections, and an unacknowledged eating disorder such as anorexia or bulimia. It occurs in diabetes when cells craving energy have no access to glucose and start burning fats and proteins instead.

- *Blurred vision.* Like being TATT or losing weight unexpectedly, blurred vision is a symptom that can be a warning for all sorts of conditions from simple failing eyesight to diseases of the nervous system. When sugar levels become high in diabetes, this can cause swelling of the lens of one or both eyes, producing blurred vision.

- *Itchy genitals.* High levels of sugar, especially in the urine (glycosuria), produce the perfect conditions in which yeasts such as thrush (*Candida albicans*) thrive. These infections will cause itching for both men and women in the most delicate places and in women can produce an intensely irritating white vaginal discharge. Glycosuria can also trigger repeated bouts of urinary infections such as cystitis.

If you get this load of symptoms all ganging up on you at once, then, although not 100 per cent certain, there's a very high chance you will be heading towards a diagnosis of diabetes. However, if even just one or two of these symptoms hang around for more than a day or so, it would be a very good idea to consult your family doctor to find out what's going on.

Type 1 diabetes

The key differentiating features of Type 1 diabetes are the younger age group it tends to affect and its rapid rate of onset, which is much faster than in Type 2.

The other classic features can helpfully be remembered as the 4 Ts, which form part of a campaign by British charity Diabetes UK to raise awareness of and so increase diagnosis of Type 1 diabetes. The Ts in question are:

- **T**oilet. This concerns polyuria and highlights the likelihood of people passing more urine than normal. In children this can mean that previously dry youngsters start wetting the bed and that babies have much heavier nappies.

- **T**hirsty. This represents the polydipsia we have looked at already.

- **T**ired. As we've seen, tiredness despite getting a good night's sleep is a common feature.

- **T**hinner. Highlights the fact that weight loss may be an early symptom.

If you or, more likely, your child has this set of symptoms, then you need to make an appointment with your family doctor to have them checked and their blood sugar tested as a matter of urgency.

Type 2 diabetes

The onset of symptoms in Type 2 tends to be much slower – over weeks and months rather than a matter of days. These symptoms are also more common in people who are overweight and over 40.

The types of symptoms to look out for are the same as those listed in the "Before diagnosis" section above and may also include slow healing of cuts and wounds. So if these symptoms (or even two or three of them together) are something you can identify with, they definitely need checking with the doctor.

Hypoglycaemia (low blood sugar)

Hypoglycaemia, or a "hypo" as it's often called, occurs when your blood sugar level drops off the bottom of the normal range (below 4 mmol/L). This means that your body has insufficient fuel to carry out some of its most basic functions and you will rapidly begin to feel unwell. Symptoms include:

- feeling hungry
- sweating
- dizziness
- sleepiness
- shakiness
- blurred vision
- racing pulse
- irritability

- poor concentration and confusion
- even feeling drunk.

If it isn't treated (by having a sugary drink or eating something sweet), hypoglycaemia can even lead to unconsciousness.

Hyperglycaemia (high blood sugar)

If blood sugar levels rise above 7 mmol/L when you haven't eaten or above 11 mmol/L two hours after a meal, they will start to cause symptoms. These are very reminiscent of those we looked at leading to an initial diagnosis of diabetes:

- tiredness
- thirst
- hunger
- frequent urination.

If not treated with medication to lower sugar levels, there's a risk that hyperglycaemia may progress to one of diabetes' most dangerous complications: ketoacidosis.

Diabetic ketoacidosis (DKA)

This is a very serious complication of diabetes, which is treated as a medical emergency. It is most common in people with Type 1 diabetes (and in rare cases can be the first sign of it), but it can also happen in Type 2.

What are the causes?

It occurs when the body is forced to use up fats to make energy because the lack, or inefficiency, of insulin has meant that cells are being starved of sugar. When fats are broken down, they produce harmful, acidic waste products called ketones. And when these combine in the blood with already high levels of sugar, the problems can start.

What are the symptoms?

Initially, the symptoms are those of diabetes itself:

- polyuria
- polydipsia
- tiredness.

As the condition progresses, these are joined by:

- dehydration (with a particularly dry mouth)
- belly aches
- shortness of breath.

And in the later stages:

- vomiting
- racing pulse
- rapid breathing
- dizziness
- confusion and disorientation
- smell of pear drops on the breath (the smell of the ketones themselves).

Beyond this stage, if the situation is not corrected, there is a real possibility of serious, life-threatening complications occurring:

- acute kidney failure
- swelling of the brain
- acute respiratory distress.

If you (or your child) develop symptoms of the early stages of DKA, you must seek medical advice immediately. If you recognize the symptoms as those of the later stages, you will need to dial 999 immediately.

3

What causes diabetes?

As we saw in Chapter 1, Type 1 and Type 2 diabetes occur for
different reasons. Type 1 results from a lack of production of
the hormone insulin in the body, whereas with Type 2 there's
a combination of both lack of insulin and the development of
resistance to its effects. And as we have seen, the other main
difference is that Type 1 most commonly develops in childhood,
whereas Type 2 generally affects people over the age of 40.

So because the conditions are slightly different entities, it's
perhaps not surprising that they have different causes. In this
chapter we will look at each type in turn.

Type 1

Type 1 diabetes is part of a group of conditions called
autoimmune diseases. They get their name because they occur
when someone's own immune system turns on them and attacks
and destroys cells or tissues in their body.

The immune system

The body's immune system is made up of a collection of tissues, organs, and cells which work collectively to protect against infection by bacteria, viruses, and fungi; they also try to keep cancer cells at bay. Our immune system has a variety of weapons and armour to deploy against these enemy bugs and germs, ranging from the physical protection offered by the outer level of our skin to form a barrier against invasion, to an army of white blood cells which can attack and kill any micro-organisms that do manage to breach our external defences and make it inside the body.

One specific variety of these white cells, called lymphocytes, helps identify and destroy invading organisms by producing antibodies (also known as immunoglobulins). These antibodies are large protein molecules that can recognize foreign cells entering the body, because they produce, or have an outer coating of, their own characteristic molecules, called antigens. The arrival of an antigen into the body triggers the production of a specific antibody to it, which will attach to the invading organism and kill it.

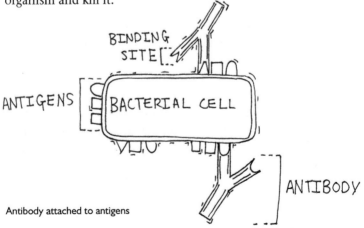

BINDING SITE

ANTIGENS

BACTERIAL CELL

ANTIBODY

Antibody attached to antigens

Autoimmune conditions

When the process above misfires, it can trigger the body to produce antibodies to bits of itself. The resulting onslaught by the immune system causes damage and even destruction of the body's own tissues, leading to a variety of possible diseases, depending on which organ is under attack.

A common example of an autoimmune disorder is rheumatoid arthritis, in which the immune attack causes chronic inflammation in joints with resultant pain, swelling, and eventually deformity.

It's not known exactly what causes the immune system to misbehave in this way, but it's believed that it might actually be the microbes it is supposed to protect against that trigger changes that stop the immune system distinguishing between healthy cells and antigens. It's also thought that some people may have a genetic predisposition which makes this more likely to happen. Either way, it's not good news and when it happens in the pancreas it leads to Type 1 diabetes.

Autoimmunity and diabetes

In Type 1 diabetes, the immune malfunction causes it to attack and kill the beta cells in the pancreas that make insulin, stopping its production. Scientists reckon that a combination of a genetic predisposition (Type 1 diabetes can run in families) and damage from a viral infection makes the immune system behave in this way.

For more detail about the biology of insulin and the pancreas, see Appendix 1.

Type 2

The causes of this type of diabetes are not quite so clear-cut. Researchers have identified a number of different risk factors that make it more likely someone will develop the condition. As you'll see, some of these are genetic, over which you will have absolutely no control, whereas others are related to lifestyle and can certainly be avoided.

Weight
Being overweight is one of the biggest risk factors for developing Type 2 diabetes. It's believed that as weight goes up, with a subsequent rise in BMI from the overweight category to full-on obesity (see Chapter 1), there is a reduction in the insulin released in the body and an increase in resistance to it, particularly in muscles and the liver. Reducing weight is known to improve the situation.

Inactivity
There is a clear relationship between lack of exercise and the development of insulin resistance. The flip side of this is that leading an active lifestyle is known to prevent insulin resistance.

Age
Here's a risk factor that you can't do anything about. Being over 45 is particularly risky when it comes to developing Type 2 diabetes. This is believed to be because as we age we become more sedentary and do less exercise and so have reduced muscle, increased fat stores, and therefore greater insulin resistance.

Family history
If you have a parent or sibling (particularly a twin) with Type 2 diabetes, then you will have an underlying predisposition to developing the condition. However, because eating habits and other important lifestyle habits such as exercise (or lack of it) tend to be similar for family members, it's often hard to know

whether the increased risk is down to these factors or because of a genetic predisposition. It's thought that it's probably a combination of the two.

Race

This is a genetic risk you will find it hard to avoid. If you are from a family of South Asian, Chinese, African-Caribbean, or black African origin, you have a higher risk of developing the disease than if your family of origin is from elsewhere on the planet.

Where Type 2 diabetes is concerned, lifestyle risk factors seem to be the biggest causes, with genetic factors playing a part too. So if you are in a high-risk category due to racial origin, it's even more important to maintain a healthy lifestyle.

Mythbuster

Eating too much sugar gives you diabetes.
Type 1 diabetes is caused by genetics and problems with the immune system, whereas family history and lifestyle factors play a part in developing Type 2. And although being overweight can trigger Type 2 in some people, this is not true for everyone and is caused by overeating fats and more complex carbohydrates and not simply sugar.

4

How is diabetes diagnosed?

If you are worried that you have developed some of the symptoms of diabetes, or think a friend or family member may have, then it's important to have your concerns checked out as soon as possible. Many pharmacies will offer quick finger-prick checks of blood sugar, which can be a useful pointer, but it's best to make an appointment to see your family doctor to have things looked at more fully.

Diabetes can also be picked up by "accident" in people with no specific warning signs for it. Usually, this happens when you are having blood tests for less specific symptoms such as persistent tiredness, general achiness, or mood changes. If an unexpectedly raised blood glucose shows up, your doctor will also want to find out about how you've been feeling lately and dig a bit deeper into your symptoms beyond those you initially consulted them about.

Seeing your family doctor

Your doctor will want to get a full picture of what's been happening to you and will no doubt come at you with a stream of questions. And it's important to remember that although to you – thanks to words of wisdom from a family member or an in-depth search of the internet – it may be barn door obvious that you have diabetes, there are other conditions that can have similar symptoms. Your doctor will need to quiz you about symptoms you may see as way off the mark, but that's because it's as important for them to rule other conditions out as it is to rule diabetes in.

The medical history

As doctors, much like police detectives, we are trained to go about our enquiries in a methodical and logical manner. So in the same way that detectives will want to interview all witnesses to a crime, even if they have a murder weapon with a suspect's fingerprints all over it, your doctor will not just hear the words "I'm tired and weeing a lot and that's what happened to my nan when she got diabetes" and jump straight to the same conclusion and immediately start treatment. So they will ask you about:

- all the symptoms you have had and the exact order in which they developed

- whether you have a family history of any medical conditions

- whether you have tried any over-the-counter treatments or home remedies to try to help your symptoms

- your drug, alcohol, and smoking history and what your normal diet is like.

Once they feel they have a handle on all of this, they will want to check you over.

The physical examination

Your doctor will want to check some basic observations: pulse, blood pressure, height and weight (to work out BMI).

At the initial assessment they may ask you to provide a urine sample so they can check for the presence of glucose, ketones, and protein, as well as tell-tale signs of infection such as the presence of red and white cells and chemicals called nitrites.

Once they have done all of this, they will be able to give you an idea of whether or not they think you have diabetes and arrange for you to have a set of blood tests to confirm their suspicions.

Blood tests

There are three main blood tests used to make a diagnosis of diabetes:

- fasting blood glucose

- oral glucose tolerance test (OGTT)

- haemoglobin A1c.

To confirm the diagnosis in people without classical symptoms, two tests need to be carried out at different times and the results of both need to fall into the abnormal "diabetic" range. Only one test is needed where symptoms are obviously present.

Fasting blood glucose

This test will involve you having an early-morning blood sample taken before you've had your first cup of tea or coffee or enjoyed your breakfast. You are likely to be advised to have nothing to eat or drink except water from around 10 p.m. the previous night. What happens next will depend on the result.

If the results are 6.1–6.9 mmol/L, you will need to have an OGTT.

If they are more than 7.0 mmol/L, they are diagnostic for diabetes.

Oral glucose tolerance test (OGTT)

Here you will once again start by having an early-morning fasting glucose blood test. You will then be asked to have a sugary drink containing 75 grammes of glucose, followed by another blood test two hours later.

This test mimics what happens after a meal, when blood sugar levels should initially rise and then settle back to normal. This isn't the case in diabetes, where sugar levels remain high, allowing the diagnosis to be made based on the results range below.

If two hours after the drink the results are 8–11.0 mmol/L, this means impaired glucose tolerance.

A result of more than 11.1 mmol/L is diagnostic of diabetes.

Haemoglobin A1c (HbA1c)

This blood test, which does not need to be taken after fasting, looks at the amount of blood sugar that has combined with the haemoglobin in the red cells in your blood. It gives an accurate idea of what the blood sugar level has been over the past two to three months. The higher the levels of glucose, the more glucose will end up attached to haemoglobin.

An HbA1c of more than 48 is diagnostic for diabetes.

Once your doctor has enough evidence to confirm the diagnosis, you will be called in to discuss what needs to happen next. This may initially involve advice on lifestyle measures that can help lower your sugar levels, or it can mean starting on medication straight away. Either way, you will be introduced to a host of different professionals who will help to ensure that you quickly start to feel better, your blood sugar is well controlled, and potential complications are spotted early.

5

Who is involved in your care?

My youngest son, Archie, is a keen little footballer who loves nothing more than to be kicking a ball about: given the chance, he would play morning, noon, and night. Fortunately for him, there are a couple of local leagues where lads his age can play football regularly, and since he was about eight, he has been part of one of the teams based near us, the Whitchurch Panthers. So every weekend he can play competitive matches and during the week, every week, he heads off to training sessions.

It's proved a wonderful opportunity for him to get fit, improve his individual skills, learn the importance of teamwork, and, most importantly, simply indulge his love of "the beautiful game". And it's paid off; he's certainly a better player than he used to be and he has a much better grasp of the tactics of the game too.

To achieve this, he has had to put in a lot of hard work. Although the training has been laid on, the kit bought, and the matches arranged, the onus is on Archie, and each of his team mates, to make the most of these opportunities, to turn up for training (come rain or shine or a desire for a lie-in), to put 100 per cent effort into their performances each game, and to wear their team's colours with pride when they are chosen to play.

Like football, diabetes care is very much a team effort. And following diagnosis you will be given the opportunity to have regular check-ups and benefit from the support of a wide variety of healthcare professionals with different areas of expertise. Everything you need will be laid on for you.

But you have to choose to engage with these people yourself, turn up for appointments (come rain or shine or a desire for a lie-in), put 100 per cent effort into following advice about treatment regimes, diet, and exercise, and take pride in your own levels of self-care. Because in the same way that Archie's coaches can get him ready for matches but can't play the game for him, these health professionals are there to help and support you, but the way your diabetes is managed is ultimately your responsibility.

Here's a look at who is out there to help and what they can do.

General practitioner (GP)

GPs are the gatekeepers to pretty much everything that happens in the NHS and know exactly who else's experience to draw on to aid them in your care. As your family doctor, they will be aware of all of the details of your health, including your medical, social, and family history, and so will be the best professional to treat you as you, an individual person, and not just Josephine Bloggs the diabetic.

It may well be that your local practice has a doctor who specializes in diabetes and who tends to look after all patients with the condition. Very often, though, it will be your usual doctor who helps coordinate the involvement of other professionals and who, most importantly, provides you with good continuity of care.

Practice nurse

You will be able to find out about your practice nurses either from your GP or by looking at the practice website or leaflet. They are nurses who are trained to help people manage long-term medical conditions such as high blood pressure, asthma, and heart disease, as well as diabetes. Some may have particular skills in treating one of these conditions.

They tend to have longer appointments than GPs and so have more time not only to check up on how you are doing, take measurements such as blood pressure and weight, and carry out blood and urine tests, but also to give practical advice and information. This can include everything from tailor-made hints about diet and exercise to showing you how to use a home blood sugar or blood pressure monitor. Some practice nurses have had extra training and so will also be able to prescribe medicines for you and adjust your treatment regime when needed.

Hospital consultant

Most local hospitals will have specialists in diabetes, usually called endocrinologists because they will also have an interest in treating a range of other hormone-related problems and not just diabetes. You may be referred to one of these specialists if your GP and practice nurse are finding your diabetes particularly tricky to control or if you develop troublesome complications of the disease. Consultants will also be involved in the routine care of children and pregnant women who develop diabetes.

They usually work in hospital outpatient clinics in teams which include junior doctors who are themselves training to be endocrinologists, and specialist nurses, and you may well be seen by one of these clinicians rather than the consultant themselves. They may just want to see you once or twice to carry out specialized tests or try you on new treatments, or because of the nature of your particular condition, they may keep you on their books for years and follow you up regularly.

Diabetic specialist nurse

These nurses have undertaken extra specialist training in all aspects of diabetes care. They are based in hospitals but will also go out and see people at home. Their roles are:

- advising and educating professional and non-professional staff caring for people with diabetes, including non-specialist doctors and nurses and family members

- working on individualized care plans with people who have diabetes

- helping in diabetes management during a crisis such as hypoglycaemia, poorly healing ulcers, or when someone has another illness

- providing extra support during periods of change of treatment or when control needs improving

- teaching about how to use diabetes equipment.

If you are being seen in hospital outpatients, you may well be introduced to a specialist nurse there, or you might be referred to one by your practice nurse.

Optician/optometrist

Diabetes is not good for your eyes and poor control can lead to conditions that can potentially affect your eyesight or even lead to blindness. (For more on this, see Chapter 9.)

It's therefore really important to have regular checks at your local optometrist so that they can keep a look out for these problems developing and refer you to a hospital eye specialist (ophthalmologist) if they see early signs of these conditions.

Throughout the UK all people over the age of 12 who have diabetes are included in the annual diabetic retinopathy screening programme and will be invited by letter for a thorough eye check to look for these changes. The tests may be carried out at a variety of locations locally, including hospitals, GP surgeries, and optician's.

Podiatrist

Podiatrists, also known as chiropodists, are trained in the diagnosis and medical and surgical treatment of conditions affecting the foot and ankle, and are skilled at picking up on complications of diabetes (see Chapter 9).

They can be accessed on the NHS in the UK if you have diabetes and will be happy to carry out an annual review and see you at any time to deal with problems that crop up. People with diabetes are at much higher risk of needing an amputation, but by keeping an eye on your feet, this risk will be greatly reduced.

Dietician

These professionals are trained in assessment, diagnosis, and treatment of problems related to all aspects of diet and nutrition. You may be referred to one by your family doctor soon after diagnosis or if management of your diabetes becomes a problem at a later stage.

They can give you tailored advice on all aspects of nutrition from tightening blood sugar control to losing weight.

Mythbuster

Type 2 diabetes is a mild form of the disease.
Neither type of diabetes is mild and you need to follow the advice of your medical team whichever type you have to avoid the potential life-limiting complications it can cause.

6

Dealing with your diabetes

Managing diabetes is a big commitment. It will not go away if you close your eyes and try to ignore it; in fact, it will get worse. And although you will always have doctors and other health professionals to help you with the task, they cannot deal with it all for you; they can only offer advice, prescriptions, and support.

The flip side of this is that if you do focus on doing your best to develop a routine for treating and monitoring it and if you turn up for appointments and screening tests, there is every chance that you won't run into problems with it. And as we'll see later in Chapter 9, those problems are many and often serious.

So a shared care approach is by far the best, with some home testing, diet, and exercise regimes being down to you, whereas other tests and checks will be carried out at the local surgery, podiatry clinic, and optometrist's. But you still have to turn up.

Home monitoring

Many people with diabetes, especially those being treated with insulin, will test their own blood sugar levels at home. It's a very effective way to monitor for symptoms of both hypo- and hyperglycaemic episodes, as well as to track the impact of lifestyle and medication changes on regulating sugar levels.

For those with Type 2 diabetes treated with diet or pills alone, the evidence of effectiveness for home testing is lacking. But although many experts suggest that people with Type 2 shouldn't test their own sugars because of its unproven benefits and lack of cost effectiveness, many diabetes charities disagree, asserting that it may be helpful for some people to keep tabs on their disease.

In the UK, glucose meters are not available via the NHS, and test strips and lancets can only be prescribed if you are on insulin. All the necessary kit can, however, be bought online and from major pharmacies. Your doctor or diabetes nurse will be happy to advise on which models are best, depending on price band and ease of use. They will also show you how and when to use them.

How it's done

For those who are squeamish about the sight of blood, and especially their own, the idea of self-testing can be a bit daunting, because you *will* see blood, albeit a small drop, and it definitely has to be yours. And you have to draw that blood yourself by plunging the tip of a sharp little lancet into the side of the tip of your finger. But don't let that put you off. As always: no pain, no gain.

You will need a blood glucose monitor, testing strips, and lancets, which your doctor and diabetes nurse will tell you how to get hold of. Next, follow these steps:

- Wash your hands with warm water, to clean them and to aid blood flow to your fingertip.
- Turn on the monitor and have a test strip ready.
- Select your finger (alternate which one you use to avoid them becoming sore).
- Use the lancet device to collect the drop of your blood.
- Place it onto the test strip.
- Read the blood glucose level on the display.

What the result means

The times and frequency of testing and the ideal figures to be looking for will be something your diabetes nurse and doctor will discuss with you.

If you have Type 1 diabetes and are on insulin, the levels should be

- 3–7 mmol/L on waking
- 4–7 mmol/L for your blood sugar level before meals
- 5–9 mmol/L 90 minutes afterwards.

With Type 2, the levels will be

- 4–7 mmol/L before meals
- less than 8.5 mmol/L two hours after.

You will be given a booklet in which to record your results to help your diabetes team to follow your progress with you. Don't panic if this all sounds a bit complicated. You will be shown exactly how to test and what you're looking for by your diabetes nurse.

Urine testing

Although blood testing is very much the gold standard test used to evaluate sugar levels accurately at home, some people may be given urine test strips to check whether their sugar has gone too high or there are chemicals called ketones in it, to identify hyperglycaemia. No urine strips can check low blood sugar.

In most cases you will need to pee onto the stick and then compare the colour change on the strip with the chart on the strip's container. You will be given a plan about what to do if it shows a particularly high level, especially if that's accompanied by the presence of high levels of ketones.

Clinic-based follow-up

Once your condition is stable, you will be invited to your local clinic or doctor's surgery every three to six months if you have Type 1 and at least once a year if you have Type 2 for a number of tests and checks. Prior to stability, this testing may happen more frequently.

The tests will look not only at blood sugar control but also at the other risk factors that can make the effects of your diabetes much worse.

Blood sugar checks

It's most likely that these checks will be carried out by a nurse who, if you are using insulin, will want to look at your home sugar monitoring diary and go through it with you to see what's been happening since you last met. He or she will then want to check what your HbA1c level is (see Chapter 4).

Ideal levels are as follows, although, as with all tests, you will have your own targets given to you by your medical team:

- People without diabetes: 20–41 mmol/mol
- People with diabetes: less than 48 mmol/mol

If your result puts you above your target level, your dose of medication can be adjusted to try to rectify things.

Blood fats and cholesterol

The main fats found in the blood are cholesterol and triglycerides. High levels of these, particularly in combination with diabetes, will increase your risk of developing heart disease.

Cholesterol itself has two forms: high density lipoprotein (HDL) and low density lipoprotein (LDL). HDL is "good" cholesterol, which can protect the heart, whereas LDL is "bad" cholesterol involved in atheroma formation.

Ideally total cholesterol should be less than 4 mmol/L, with HDL more than 1.0 mmol/L in men and 1.2mmol/L in women; LDL should be less than 2.0mmol/L.

If your levels of "bad" and total cholesterol are much more than this, you may be advised to start medication to lower them. This decision is most likely to be based not just on cholesterol levels but on what's called your Q risk.

This is a calculation based on figures for your blood sugar, cholesterol, blood pressure, age, sex, and BMI, which produces a percentage risk of developing heart disease in the next ten years. A result of more than 10 per cent will suggest that treatment to lower cholesterol should be started.

Blood pressure (BP)

The blood in our body needs to be pumped around under pressure; otherwise, it would just slosh around inside and never carry oxygen to our brain or extremities. Unfortunately, you can have too much of a good thing and high blood pressure puts you at risk of having a heart attack or stroke and sustaining kidney damage.

The readings that doctors and nurses make of your BP give two results:

- one in systole, the technical term for when the heart muscle contracts to pump blood out
- and the other in diastole, which is the relaxation phase before the next pump.

They're recorded as systolic level/diastolic level.

All of us, diabetic or not, have an ideal level for our blood pressure, but in diabetes it needs to be even more tightly controlled because of the way it adds to the risk of complications. The guidelines depend on whether you have Type 1 or Type 2.

Type 1
The general target for people with Type 1 is a level below 135/85. If there is any protein in the urine suggesting kidney damage or other complications, then the target drops to lower than 130/80.

Type 2
Here, the general target is slightly more generous at less than 140/80. Again, if complications develop, that drops to 130/80.

High blood pressure (hypertension) can be treated with a number of different prescription medicines. But there is also evidence that you can help keep it down yourself by:

- eating less salt
- eating those famous five portions of fruit and veg each day
- getting some exercise
- keeping your weight to a healthy level
- not exceeding recommended limits of alcohol.

Kidney function

Given the risk that diabetes poses to your kidneys, your kidney function will be checked at least annually by taking a blood test and sending off a urine sample to analyse levels of protein. Abnormalities may mean that treatment needs to be started or simply that monitoring will become more frequent.

Checks of eyes and feet

These checks will be carried out at least annually, depending on their outcome.

Eyes

It's important for everyone with diabetes to have their eyes examined regularly by an optician to check for general deterioration and early signs of diabetic complications. In the UK there is also a diabetic retinopathy screening programme which everyone with diabetes will be invited to participate in. These checks involve the use of high-definition retinal cameras to obtain photos of your retina that can be compared year by year to monitor for change.

Feet

Diabetes nurses will carry out checks of basic foot health at your annual review, where they will poke you to check for sensation and feel for your pulses. It is also advisable to have regular reviews with a podiatrist as well.

Individual care plan

Although this mainly refers to people with Type 1 diabetes, those with Type 2 (particularly if on insulin) will also receive education about the best ways to manage their diabetes at home and the issues that can crop up that need medical attention.

 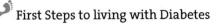

General education and nutritional advice

This will be a one-to-one run-through of much of the advice contained in this book. It will be tailor-made to your particular circumstances, though. So if you are a shift worker, have other medical conditions affecting diet and exercise (e.g. coeliac disease), or have religious beliefs that affect your diabetes (e.g. fasting in Ramadan), you will know how to adapt your treatment for yourself, rather than trying to follow off-the-peg advice meant for all.

Advice on insulin

You will have a regime to follow that allows you to adapt your dose according to changing circumstances, such as illness, and in response to blood sugar levels. You will also be advised about where on your body to inject and how to rotate to different sites in order to avoid one of the most common complications of injecting: lipohypertrophy.

This is caused when repeated injections at the same site make fatty lumps appear and the skin become stiffer. If insulin is injected into these lumpy areas, its absorption is much slower and this can trigger hypos.

Warning signs for hypos

Your plan will include details of how to spot a hypo and what to do if you have one. It will advise you to have some of the remedies always to hand:

- sugary drinks (cola/fruit juice)
- a handful of sugary sweets such as jelly babies
- glucose gel, which can be prescribed.

Contact details

A list of who to contact and when if you run into problems. This will range from booking a routine doctor's appointment to dialling 999.

 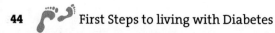

7

Lifestyle modifications

To give yourself the best chance of keeping your diabetes under control, you need to play a full part in your own treatment by making some changes to your diet and lifestyle. Diabetes is best managed in collaboration with healthcare professionals, where you and they are all part of a team; it is not something that is simply done by them to you.

As we'll see in Chapter 9, the long-term consequences of poorly controlled diabetes have the potential to be quite horrendous. And the odds of getting into trouble are increased by a life without activity, fuelled by a diet that's high in fat and sugar, washed down with a generous volume of alcohol, and rounded off with a puff on the odd cigarette or two.

You may have what you already consider to be the perfect diet and an exercise regime that rivals the training schedule of Mo Farah, but what follows may still have the odd little nugget of advice that you will find helpful. If, however, you are largely sofa-bound with a cupboard full of cola, crisps, and confectionary, then there will be useful tips galore for you.

Whatever your lifestyle – and it's probably somewhere between these two extremes – these suggestions aren't there to turn your life into a boot camp with bland, basic rations, but they have been shown to help. And given the risks to your general health from poorly controlled blood sugar levels, they have to be worth a try.

Diet in Type 1 diabetes

A balanced, healthy diet needs to contain a mixture of proteins, fats, sugars and carbohydrates, vitamins, and minerals. In Type 1 diabetes, care needs to be taken about which types of these food groups are eaten, alongside the amount of each, but a special "diabetic" diet is not recommended. And please do not fork out money on "diabetic" foods; they really aren't necessary.

In general, your diet should be low in saturated fats and high in fibre and have at least five portions per day of fruit and vegetables. It's also important to have three meals spread out through the day, including a good breakfast.

Carbohydrates

This group of foods contains all of the large molecules which, when digested, are broken down into their smaller constituent sugars ready for absorption. All carbohydrates increase blood sugar levels.

Examples of foods containing carbohydrates are:

- rice, pasta, bread
- potatoes (chips/crisps/jackets included)
- cakes, biscuits, sweets
- fruit
- dairy products such as milk and yoghurt.

The effect these will have on your blood sugar will depend on how much of each you eat and drink, the dose of your insulin, and how much you burn off by exercising. Getting the balance right can be tricky, as it will be very individual – some will exercise more than others whereas some will indulge a bigger appetite. Your doctor, diabetes nurse, and dietician will be able to help tailor a regime for you and, if you have Type 1, will probably teach you how to accurately count your carbohydrate intake.

Fats

We all need some fats in our diet but they are high in calories and some, called saturated fats, put us at increased risk of developing atherosclerosis (furring up of the arteries). It's a good idea then to avoid foods that are high in these, such as:

- butter, cream, cheese
- meat and meat products (sausage rolls, burgers, hot dogs)
- cakes, biscuits, pies, pasties
- pizzas, chip-shop chips.

All foods bought in shops and supermarkets in the UK have labels highlighting their nutritional content. These are coded like traffic lights: red means the level contained is high, orange denotes medium, and green is low. Always try to avoid those where the saturated fat level is highlighted in red. As with traffic lights, it signals stop!

More tips for a low-fat diet

- Buy low-fat varieties of milk (skimmed or semi-skimmed), cheese, mince, bacon, etc. Supermarkets will stock all of these and they are just as tasty.
- Trim the fat off bacon and take the skin off chicken.
- Cook with low fat vegetable oils and hold off on the lard, butter, and goose fat (unless it's Christmas).
- Have your coffees "skinny" and buy low-calorie or zero-sugar fizzy drinks and juices.
- Limit takeaways to treats rather than making them a regular occurrence – no matter how great they taste, they frequently have a very high fat content.

Diet in Type 2 diabetes

Very similar rules to those above apply if you have Type 2 diabetes. It's always best to have a healthy, balanced diet, low in fat, high in fibre, and with five portions of fruit and veg per day. Apologies for being repetitive but we all need reminding, and the need for this regime is pricking my conscience too.

In Type 2, a healthy diet is not only important to help control blood sugar levels, but it is also an excellent way to help lose weight, another key to controlling this type of diabetes. So:

- keep saturated fat intake low (see above)
- have sweets and cakes as an occasional treat and choose low-calorie drinks and juices
- do your best to have five portions of fruit and veg per day
- eat around two portions of oily fish per week, such as sardines and salmon; if you are vegetarian or vegan, you can get a healthy dose of these omega 3 oils from flaxseed and rapeseed oils and walnuts

- reduce portion sizes by using a smaller plate and half filling it with vegetables. Don't go for second helpings.

Alcohol

Just because you have diabetes, it doesn't mean that you can't enjoy the odd pint of beer or two with your mates or partake in a nice glass of vino from time to time. You obviously need to follow the general guidance about safe limits for drinking (14 units per week for women and 21 for men), but with diabetes, alcohol also brings the risk of triggering hypos.

To avoid this, don't go out drinking on an empty stomach and when you get in have some toast, cereal, biscuits, or other carbs before you head off to bed. This last piece of advice is vital, as you can still develop a hypo the morning after the night before if you don't, with this risk lasting for up to 16 hours after you've swallowed your last drop of booze.

Exercise

This is one of those subjects that all healthcare professionals will waffle on about like bores whenever we are given the chance, because it is, without doubt, one of the most important components of a healthy lifestyle for everyone on the planet, whether they have diabetes or not. There is no shortage of hard, scientific evidence to back up the fact that regular physical exercise can reduce everyone's risk of developing:

- heart disease and stroke
- colon and breast cancer
- osteoarthritis and hip fractures
- depression and dementia.

And if that's not enough, it even boosts your chances of avoiding an early death by 30 per cent.

Exercise benefits in diabetes

On top of its life-giving benefits for everyone, engaging in some sort of exercise also pays specific dividends if you have diabetes.

- Cells become more sensitive to insulin.

- Blood sugar levels are lowered by mechanisms that avoid the need for insulin.

- The levels of cholesterol and other blood fats (such as triglycerides) are lowered.

- It improves blood pressure levels.

- It can help with weight loss.

This combination therefore not only improves blood sugar control but also helps prevent many of the complications diabetes can lead to.

What's involved?

The current guidelines advise us all to get 150 minutes of aerobic exercise each week. This means doing something active for at least half an hour each day to raise your pulse rate and make you work up a bit of a sweat.

These activities do not need to be gym-based, involve the immense cost of joining a sports club, or warrant purchasing anything made of lycra, unless, of course, you want to. Varying what you do is most likely to make you stick to your routine without becoming bored stiff by doing the same activity day in and day out. And if you're a sociable person, or someone who needs company to stay motivated, choose an exercise that is done in pairs or teams.

The list of suitable options obviously includes most sports, from football and netball to badminton and judo (although perhaps not darts and snooker), the exercises on offer at a gym, as well as more general leisure activities such as brisk walks, swimming, cycling, gardening, and DIY.

So although your age and any other medical conditions may well dictate which of the above you physically can and can't do, there really is no excuse for doing nothing.

Before getting started

Although they will no doubt give you the go-ahead, it's worth running your desire to go out and get active past your doctor or diabetes nurse. As they will know about your general health and the way your diabetes affects you as an individual, they will be well placed to advise you about the types of exercise that will suit you, how to get started, and how you might need to adjust your diabetes treatment in the light of your new burst of activity.

This adjustment is particularly necessary if you have Type 1 diabetes because of the effects that exercise has on blood sugar and insulin sensitivity. You might, for example, need to check blood sugar levels before engaging in activity and then adjust your insulin dose according to the result. And you might be advised to carry some carbs with you to raise blood sugar quickly if needed.

Other considerations are choice of injection site of insulin, as this can affect the rate at which it is absorbed into your system, and the time of day that you engage in exercise, which will have a bearing on when you eat your main meals.

With Type 2 diabetes, unless it's treated with insulin, you won't have to make any adjustments to medication before starting out. The really good news is that by combining a decent amount of exercise with an ideal diet, some people with Type 2 diabetes can experience their diabetes being reversed. This can mean they are advised to stop their medication, and their risk of getting any long-term complications is dramatically reduced. That has got to be worth the sweat of doing some exercise.

Smoking

If you have diabetes, the last thing you want to do is start smoking, and if you already smoke, the first thing you want to do if you develop diabetes is stop. The mathematics of the situation is very straightforward:

DIABETES + SMOKING = SERIOUSLY BAD NEWS

There's a lot of evidence to suggest that smoking makes the complications of diabetes (which we will look at in Chapter 9) far more likely to happen. In fact, studies have found that the combination of smoking with diabetes makes those complications 14 times more likely to happen than if you just smoke or have diabetes and don't smoke.

Here's a quick look at what you're more likely to be letting yourself in for if you have diabetes and continue to smoke:

- heart attacks and strokes
- kidney failure
- nerve damage
- poor circulation to your legs and feet with added risk of amputation
- premature death.

All of which helps explain the term "dying for a cigarette". And that's without even mentioning the lung diseases and cancer you are also potentially setting yourself up for if you smoke, whether you have diabetes or not.

The advice is incredibly simple: stop smoking!

But it is far more easily said than done. As any smoker (and non-deluded nurse and doctor) knows, unless you really want to stop, there is no way you will be able to.

There are many sources of help for those who do, including psychological support, nicotine replacement therapies, and medications to stop the cravings, all of which are worth exploring. There's more detail about where to find help to quit smoking in my book *First Steps out of Smoking*, also available from Lion Hudson.

People with diabetes should eat "diabetic" foods.
Foods labelled specifically for people with diabetes are found in supermarkets and large pharmacies. Not only are they unnecessary, but they are often high in calories from fats and therefore not so healthy after all. A well-balanced diet of "ordinary foods" is best.

 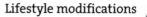

8

Medical treatments

Nurses and doctors have at their disposal a wide range of pills and injections designed to reduce the high blood levels of glucose that occur in diabetes. And the list of options continues to increase thanks to ongoing research into the disease.

Unfortunately, none of these medicines can cure either Type 1 or Type 2 diabetes and, as the condition progresses, the treatments may have to change, either by increasing the dose of a drug you are already on or by adding in more treatments.

Here's a quick run-through of what's available, who the treatments might suit, and the downside of each medicine.

Pills for diabetes

Oral medications for diabetes are used for treating people who have Type 2. They have a number of different ways of working to improve blood sugar levels and will be tried in a particular order, with new tablets being added until good control is achieved.

Metformin

This will often be the first pill given to people diagnosed with Type 2 diabetes, particularly those who are overweight, and can be prescribed alongside other medicines, including insulin.

How does it work?

It has three different actions, which combine to lower the level of glucose in the bloodstream:

- It reduces the amount of glucose absorbed from the guts after eating a meal.

- It makes muscles more sensitive to insulin so they are better at using up blood glucose.

- It cuts down the amount of glucose produced by the liver.

How is it taken?

It comes as both standard-release and modified-release tablets and as a powder which is dissolved in water and drunk. It is important to take each of these versions of the drug at the time advised each day.

Are there potential problems with it?

The most common side effects are all experienced in the digestive system and include nausea, vomiting, diarrhoea, and a metallic taste in the mouth. If these symptoms are severe, you should tell your doctor. Other side effects can include weight loss and reduced absorption of vitamin B12 (the level of this vitamin will be measured each time you have a blood test to make sure your level isn't dropping).

It is not suitable for people who have kidney disease and may also need to be avoided in people with liver disease, lung disease, and heart failure. It is, however, known to be safe in pregnancy.

Sulphonylureas

Next in the armoury of medicines for Type 2 diabetes is this group of drugs which includes gliclazide, glibenclamide, tolbutamide, and glipizide. These are often added to people's treatments when metformin alone isn't working but are sometimes used as a first-line treatment if metformin is unsuitable.

How do they work?

These drugs act on cells in the pancreas called beta cells to make them release more insulin; they also help to make insulin work more effectively around the body.

How are they taken?

They are usually taken either once or twice each day, depending on whether they are standard or modified release, either just before or with food.

Are there potential problems with them?

As with metformin, this group of drugs can cause side effects in the bowels and stomach, including nausea, diarrhoea, and flatulence. They can also cause skin rashes, weight gain, and headaches.

Their biggest potential side effect, though, is hypoglycaemia (dangerously low blood sugar). At its most severe, this can cause unconsciousness, fits, and even death, and so is a medical emergency. (There is more on hypoglycaemia in Chapter 2.)

Because of this risk of hypoglycaemia, these drugs aren't generally recommended for:

- older people
- people with kidney disease

- those working at heights or operating heavy machinery
- people who live alone or who have solitary hobbies such as hillwalking.

Pregnant and breastfeeding women should not take this group of drugs.

They are safe to take for all other people and their effects will be closely monitored by your doctor and practice nurse.

Pioglitazone

This drug is part of a group of medicines called glitazones. Other drugs in this group have been withdrawn in the past because of a possible link to liver damage and heart attacks. But pioglitazone has not been linked to either of these problems and continues to be prescribed as a treatment for Type 2 diabetes.

How does it work?

It helps to control blood sugar levels by increasing the effectiveness of the body's own insulin. This makes muscle and fat cells more efficient at taking up glucose from the blood.

How is it taken?

Pioglitazone comes as a once-daily tablet in two different strengths. The dose will be altered according to how well it seems to be working. It is usually taken alongside other diabetes medicines such as metformin.

Are there potential problems with it?

Although it has avoided the links to liver and heart disease that other glitazones have been associated with, pioglitazone hasn't got away scot-free and has recently had a controversy of its own with studies linking it to an increased risk of developing bladder cancer.

However, a large-scale study of 200,000 patients, published in July 2015 in the *Journal of the American Medical Association*, found no evidence of an increased risk of bladder cancer in people they followed up for ten years. There was, however, a small increased risk of developing prostate and pancreatic cancers for those taking the drug, and the study team reported that this needs further investigation.

More common problems with pioglitazone include minor side effects of ankle swelling and weight gain. And they are not suitable for people at risk of developing heart failure or who are susceptible to fracturing their bones. As with all medicines, your doctor will discuss the risks and benefits to you as an individual before advising you to take them.

Gliptins
This fairly new group of drugs for Type 2 diabetes includes sitagliptin and saxagliptin. They are usually prescribed to people for whom other diabetes pills don't work, or they can be added to treatment with metformin or sulphonylureas.

How do they work?
This is a bit complex because they don't affect insulin directly but trigger a chain reaction of chemical events that does. Their technical name is DPP-4 inhibitors and they block the effects of an enzyme (funnily enough called DPP-4) which breaks down hormones in the gut called incretins.

These incretins have the job of stimulating the release of insulin and blocking the release of glucagon when we have a meal. So by stopping incretins from being broken down, the gliptins improve insulin production and consequently blood sugar control.

How are they taken?
They come in tablet form and are taken once or twice per day depending on which gliptin is prescribed.

Are there potential problems with them?
The most commonly experienced side effects are mild digestive upset, skin rashes, and flu-like symptoms. They can also, more rarely, cause pancreatitis, which is inflammation of the pancreas gland and which shows up as severe upper abdominal pain with nausea and vomiting. By and large, though, they are very well tolerated by most people.

Acarbose
This drug is rarely used now because of the side effects it tends to cause and because it's not nearly as effective as the newer medications for Type 2 diabetes. It can be used along with other diabetic medicines and may be needed if other drugs aren't suitable.

How does it work?
Acarbose has a completely different mode of action to all of the other pills we have come across. Rather than trying to stimulate or help insulin to control blood sugar, it stops large carbohydrate molecules being broken down into glucose in the intestines. This means there is less glucose to be absorbed into the bloodstream in the first place.

How is it taken?
It is taken three times a day at the start of each meal. The dose will depend on your weight and may be increased over time depending on how effective it's being.

Are there potential problems with it?

The simple answer is yes! The carbohydrates that aren't broken down and absorbed in the small bowel are eventually dealt with by bacteria further down in the gut. This can often cause abdominal pain, diarrhoea, and production of rather a lot of noxious gas! As a result it is very rarely a first-line treatment these days!

Meglitinides

Finally, there are the meglitinide drugs called nateglinide and mitiglinide. These are designed to reduce the rapid rise in blood sugar that happens after eating a meal and are particularly useful for people with Type 2 diabetes who have meals at irregular times because of their work patterns.

How do they work?

They are designed to stimulate production of insulin from the pancreas at meal times.

How are they taken?

They come in tablet form in three different dose strengths which can be adjusted by your doctor according to the response you have. They are taken three times per day just before each main meal and shouldn't be taken if you miss a meal.

Are there potential problems?

Like most tablets, this group of drugs can cause digestive upsets such as heartburn, nausea, and diarrhoea. They can also cause weight gain and, because of their swift action after eating, can make some people prone to hypos.

Injectable drugs

There are two main injectable drugs for diabetes other than insulin. These are called exenatide and liraglutide.

How do they work?

They both increase insulin production when blood sugar levels are high, while reducing glucose release from the liver.

How are they taken?

Exenatide is injected twice daily, whereas liraglutide only needs to be injected once. Both come in pre-filled injection pens.

Are there potential problems?

These drugs can also cause digestive side effects as well as headaches. Exenatide can cause weight loss, and 1 per cent of those who use liraglutide have the unfortunate side effect of toothache. Neither is safe in pregnancy.

Insulin

This is the big one when it comes to the treatment of diabetes, and the therapy that most people will have heard of. In fact, for people with Type 1 diabetes, who don't make their own insulin naturally, getting regular doses of this stuff is essential. And for those with Type 2 it can also be a life-saver if the pills we've looked at above aren't effective on their own or cause unmanageable side effects and have to be stopped.

When working as it should, the body releases insulin from the pancreas in harmony with the naturally fluctuating levels of blood sugar that follow meals, snacks, cups of tea and coffee, and all the other sweets, treats, and tipples we enjoy every day. In order to try to mimic what the body does naturally, drug companies have developed different forms of insulin injection which work at different times and rates.

Insulin injections

The five main types are:

- rapid acting
- short acting
- intermediate acting
- long acting
- mixed (short and intermediate acting insulins in one syringe)

In a *First Steps* book it is impossible to go into depth about the ins and outs of these forms of insulin, but the table opposite gives an overview of how they differ and a guide to their uses.

Your doctor or nurse will adjust the doses of each of these types of insulin, depending on the response they produce on your blood sugar levels, which you will need to monitor yourself. When you are started on insulin, they will explain not only how to use, inject, and alter your insulin dose, but also how to monitor it effectively. You will also be reviewed regularly to help you avoid running into problems.

Insulin pumps

For those who have trouble managing their diabetes with the various injections available, it may be possible to use an insulin pump (although they are expensive and may require you to access special funding). These gadgets, which are about the size of a mobile phone, are worn permanently (although they can easily be taken off to take a shower or go for a swim), allowing you to receive a steady infusion of insulin which you can adjust around meals and overnight.

Type	Examples	Onset	Duration	Main use
Rapid acting	Humalog, Novorapid	10–30 minutes	3–5 hours	Taken at mealtimes, they keep the blood sugar controlled immediately after. Too high a dose risks hypos, though.
Short acting	Actrapid	30–60 minutes	4–8 hours	These are also taken at mealtimes but act more slowly than the newer rapid-acting insulins.
Intermediate acting	Humulin N, Novolin N	2 hours	18–24 hours	These are injected once or twice per day and are often used together with short-acting insulins.
Long acting	Lantus, Levemir	2 hours	24 hours	These are usually given as twice-a-day injections. They have a very low risk of causing hypos.
Mixed	Humulin 70/30, Novolog 70/30	30 minutes	Up to 24 hours	These are combinations of short- and intermediate-acting insulins in the same syringe, which make life easier as fewer injections are needed.

There are two main downsides to using pumps: they can cause soreness and skin infections at the site where they are attached with a needle, and there is a risk of ketoacidosis if the pump stops working while being worn, as it only uses rapid-acting insulin.

Help with obesity

Obesity is one of the major risk factors for Type 2 diabetes, and treating it can settle symptoms. So your diabetes team will be very keen to help you lose weight if you fall into this category.

General advice about a healthy low-fat, high-fibre diet will help with this, providing it's followed. And there's good evidence that joining organizations such as Slimming World and Weight Watchers can also help shift excess pounds. Combine that with the recommended five-times-a-week exercise regime and chances are you will be able to lose the obese tag altogether and your diabetes will improve.

Unfortunately, things are not always that simple and for some, no matter what they seem to try, the scales just don't shift. For those who aren't just kidding themselves by following every salad with a cream-cake chaser, medical help is at hand in the form of a drug called orlistat (marketed as Xenical).

How does it work?
Orlistat inhibits the chemical enzymes that break down fats in your stomach. Instead of being absorbed, they are passed out of your body. It only prevents around one-third of fats being absorbed so needs to be taken alongside a low-fat diet.

How is it taken?
It is made in capsule form and needs to be taken just before or just after every meal, washed down with a glass of water. You need to take one capsule three times per day, every day, for it to work.

Are there potential problems?
The most frequently experienced side effect is the production of loose, oily, floaty stools. This happens most commonly in people

who think the tablets can do all the work and don't change their diet. So don't cheat and it should be fine.

If you need insulin to treat Type 2 diabetes, you've not looked after yourself properly.
Diabetes tends to get worse over time and with Type 2 your body can become progressively less sensitive to the tablets used to treat it. At this point, insulin is vital for keeping your blood sugar levels under control.

9

Long-term implications

Mary Poppins may have waxed lyrical about how a "spoonful of sugar helps the medicine go down", but if you have diabetes, you need to ensure that your spoonful of medicine helps your sugar go down. Poorly controlled diabetes with persistently raised levels of sugar pumping around your circulation will not do you any favours.

Diabetes is very unforgiving if you don't treat it with the respect it demands. If you give it an inch, it will take a toe, or your eyesight, or your life far sooner than you would like it to. High levels of unregulated sugar in the blood are potentially very damaging to your organs, and given that this sugar is circulating throughout your body, the damage can be widespread.

In this chapter we will take a top-to-toe look at the risks posed by poorly controlled diabetes – not to be alarmist for the sake of it, but because in my line of work I have frequently seen the havoc that unfettered diabetes can wreak. And it ain't pretty. So forgive me if what follows is not sugar-coated.

Eyes

As my nan always said to me and my brother if we were waving sticks around near each other's heads, "Be careful: you only get one pair of eyes." Diabetes does not need careless, make-believe swordplay to cause damage to the eyes; it can do it all by itself and in a couple of ways: by making cataracts more likely in the lenses at the front of the eye and by affecting the retina at the back.

Cataracts

Cataracts affect the lenses in the eyes and it's the lenses that allow us to see and to focus on what we are looking at. Normally completely clear so as to let light pass through unimpeded and produce sharp images, they become misty, cloudy, and opaque when cataracts develop.

And although cataracts can happen to anyone, they develop earlier and progress more quickly if you have diabetes, causing a heap of symptoms such as:

- cloudy vision

- blurred vision

- yellowing of the vision

- spots in the visual field

- seeing halo patterns around lights.

Thankfully, they can be treated surgically with a straightforward day-case procedure carried out under local anaesthetic. The lens with the cataract inside is removed from the capsule that the lens sits in and is replaced by a perfectly clear, man-made lens instead.

Retinopathy

The retina is the layer of cells at the back of the eye onto which the lens focuses the images you are looking at. When the light from these images hits the retina, it is converted into electrical signals which are then conducted along nerve cells to the brain, creating a picture of what's in front of you.

Because these cells are very active, they need a good blood supply to provide the oxygen and energy required to keep them working. But too much sugar flowing through them can cause damage to these vessels, which in turn damages the retina and can lead to blindness.

Retinopathy is the most common form of eye disease to affect people with diabetes. It is also the most common cause of blindness in working-age adults.

There are three types of retinopathy:

- *Background retinopathy*. Here there are signs of damage to the retina visible to an optometrist or eye specialist, but they aren't causing you any symptoms. This damage is caused by a combination of blocked, leaky, and swollen blood vessels and will need regular monitoring to make sure it doesn't get worse.

- *Maculopathy*. The macula is a small area of light-receptor cells close to the centre of the retina which provides us with most of our central and colour vision and our ability to see fine detail. Damage to blood vessels around the macula can cause them to leak, which produces swelling and eventually scarring in this part of the retina, with subsequent loss of vision.

- *Proliferative retinopathy*. This is the body's failed attempt to restore a blood supply to the retina when existing blood vessels become damaged by growing new ones. Unfortunately, these are weak and not up to the job. They bleed very easily, which scars the retina and consequently shrinks it. This in turn can cause the retina to become detached from the back of the eye altogether.

Although background retinopathy can be stopped in its tracks by improving diabetic control, once maculopathy has developed it is likely to need laser treatment to seal the leaking blood vessels and reduce the swelling. Proliferative retinopathy is also treated using lasers, but in its more advanced stages might need treatment either with injections into the eye or even surgery.

Heart and circulation

Diabetes carries increased risks of damage to the heart itself as well as the network of blood vessels through which it pumps your blood. Of these, the vessels around your brain and around your extremities, especially your feet, are most susceptible to problems caused by this damage.

The heart

Having diabetes makes it more likely that you'll develop a heart condition. The most recent National Diabetes Audit in the UK found that people with diabetes have a:

- 71.3 per cent increased risk of angina (chest pain)
- 48.0 per cent increased risk of heart attack
- 64.9 per cent increased risk of heart failure (when the heart doesn't pump as it should, causing shortness of breath and reducing mobility).

Normally, heart disease is caused by the damage done to blood vessel walls by a combination of high blood pressure, smoking, and high cholesterol in the diet. Add high blood sugar into this cocktail and you're even more likely to have fatty deposits, called atheroma, building up inside the blood vessels. This "furs them up", reducing blood flow to the organs they supply. When the organ concerned is the heart, the poor blood supply starves the heart muscle of oxygen, causing pain on exertion (angina) or a full-on heart attack if the vessel blocks completely.

Circulation

This build-up of atheroma can happen all over the body, producing the same reduction in blood flow and oxygen supply. Its effects will depend on which part of the body is affected, with the brain and legs developing the most frequently seen problems:

- *Brain*. Reduced circulation in the brain can make a type of dementia called vascular dementia more likely, especially when the build-up is gradual and affects areas of the brain involved in memory. Sudden problems with blood flow can lead to transient ischaemic attacks (TIAs) or full-on strokes. In TIAs, the disruption to blood flow can produce temporary problems with speech or movement which resolve completely over the course of 24 hours. In strokes, the effects are permanent.

- *Legs*. Deterioration in blood supply can cause a symptom called claudication. This shows up as pain in the calf muscles which develops when walking. It settles with rest but will return during exercise. Prolonged reduction in circulation makes leg ulcers a real possibility, and it's when these don't heal that you can develop gangrene and maybe need amputation. In the UK there are 135 diabetes-related amputations each week, and in the USA the figure is more than ten times higher.

Kidneys

Moving down the body a fraction, we hit the kidneys, which also have a very unhappy relationship with diabetes. Chronic kidney disease (nephropathy) is more common in people who have diabetes and, once again, this has a lot to do with damaged blood vessels.

The kidneys are a key component in the body's waste disposal system. They are so vital to our survival that we have two of them in case one packs up.

Our blood is passed through them many times every day so that waste chemicals can be filtered out and turned into urine. It's thought that they deal with around 180 litres of blood per day in the average healthy adult, equivalent to just over two full baths.

For this process to work efficiently, the kidneys need a good blood supply and fully functioning blood vessels. As we've seen already, though, diabetes is not conducive to having healthy blood vessels.

Over time, the furred-up and leaky vessels that can develop around the kidneys due to diabetes, particularly if it's not well controlled, will significantly reduce kidney function. And poor kidney function can cause all sorts of difficulties:

- weight loss and poor appetite
- swollen ankles, feet, or hands (due to water retention)
- shortness of breath
- an increased need to urinate, particularly at night
- itchy skin
- muscle cramps
- high blood pressure (hypertension)
- nausea.

Left untreated, the toxic waste chemicals that are no longer being filtered will continue to build up in the blood and you will feel very ill indeed.

In order to cut down on the risk of sustaining kidney damage from your diabetes, you will have regular blood and urine tests to check for it. If a deterioration is discovered, then you may be prescribed drugs called angiotensin converting enzyme (ACE) inhibitors, or their cousins, the angiotensnin II receptor antagonists. These drugs lower blood pressure and protect the kidneys from further damage.

If things become uncontrollable, then you may need to have kidney dialysis. Here, your blood is "cleaned" of toxins and excess fluid is removed either by using the inside lining of your own abdomen as a filter (peritoneal dialysis), or a machine in a hospital day unit (haemodialysis). The only permanent solution, though, is to have a kidney transplant.

Nerves

Having diabetes can truly get on your nerves and it's thought that between 60 and 70 per cent of people with diabetes will eventually develop nerve damage (neuropathy). It becomes more likely the longer you have had the disease and is more common if you have poor control of your blood sugar, blood pressure, and cholesterol.

Symptom-wise, some people do get away scot-free, but most will experience pain, tingling, and numbness in the hands and feet, which can gradually spread up the arms. These symptoms are said to follow a "glove and stocking" distribution because they affect areas of the body that would be covered by a pair of gloves or long pair of socks. The technical term for this collection of nerve effects is peripheral neuropathy.

Internal organs can be affected as well, with symptoms of diarrhoea or constipation, difficulties urinating, nausea, problems with balance, dizziness on standing, and loss of sexual function.

Your doctor can prescribe medicines to help with these troublesome symptoms, with the drugs duloxetine and pregabalin being particularly effective at helping with peripheral neuropathy. But the best advice is to try to avoid developing neuropathy in the first place by taking better care of your diabetes.

Feet

The combination of both nerve damage and poor circulation that can result from diabetes can be pretty tough on your feet. A small break in the skin – for instance, from a shoe that has rubbed – can rapidly lead to the development of a foot ulcer because the numbness of your feet initially stops you feeling the first warning sign of pain. Infection can then set in, and before you know it, there's a deep hole in your skin that needs antibiotics and months of dressing by the nurse.

It's really important that you don't ignore any signs of infection in broken skin. Without timely treatment, it can rapidly lead to the development of gangrene, for which there is really only one cure: amputation.

Sexual function

If there's one possible complication that will get the attention of young men with diabetes, it's this one. I had a patient who had been diagnosed two years earlier but who had not attended check-ups or monitored his sugars, and only randomly swallowed the pills he'd been prescribed. He worked away, so it was "difficult" to attend appointments.

Then one day he noticed he couldn't sustain an erection. And when it happened again and led to the break-up of his fledgling relationship, he couldn't book an appointment fast enough.

When he discovered it was due to his diabetes, he never missed a check-up on his condition again.

Where men with diabetes are concerned, one in three can experience erectile dysfunction. Again, this is caused by damage to both nerves and blood vessels, this time to the penis, causing mechanical malfunction despite psychological and emotional desire.

The good news is that it can be treated with various pills (such as Viagra), vacuum pumps, and injections. The even better news is that it can be prevented with good control of blood sugar and blood pressure, alongside a healthy diet and active lifestyle.

Reduced blood flow and nerve damage can also affect sexual function in women. Both sensation and lubrication can be reduced, making sex painful. High sugar levels in the blood and urine can also make thrush and urine infections much more likely.

Again, good control of diabetes is key here, and chat to your nurse or doctor about the various creams and lubricants around to help make things easier, more comfortable, and therefore enjoyable with your partner.

Mythbuster

Diabetes makes you more likely to pick up colds and other illnesses.
This simply isn't true. The risk of someone with diabetes becoming unwell with a virus is no different to someone without it. However, it is recommended that you have an annual flu jab if you have diabetes because this type of infection can upset your sugar levels and put you at higher risk of developing the complications of flu.

10

Special circumstances

Diabetes of either type has different long-term implications for people depending on their age and stage of life. It affects children differently to those diagnosed with it in older age and can lead to particular problems during pregnancy.

As diabetes develops, the complications it can cause may lead to potential restrictions on lifestyle and independence, with regulations about continued driving being a particular issue for many. But as my gran (and no doubt yours) used to say, forewarned is forearmed, so in this chapter we will look at what these potential problems are in the hope that even if they can't be avoided, their impact can be minimized.

Childhood diabetes

For parents, having your child diagnosed with any illness is upsetting. It can be bad enough watching over them during a sleepless night of raging earache, or if they're nursing a fracture after coming off second best while larking about in the playground. So to have a doctor tell you they have developed a condition that will affect them throughout their lives is extremely tough.

And although many children will "grow out" of other well-known chronic conditions such as asthma or eczema, diabetes will accompany them to the grave. And at diagnosis I've seen parents who were petrified that that grave was not far off. I hope that what follows will make the situation seem less scary as it provides advice about what's ahead for youngsters and their families.

How common is it?

Figures from charity Diabetes UK for 2015 suggest that there are around 31,500 children and adolescents who have been diagnosed with diabetes in the United Kingdom, of whom 95.1 per cent have Type 1 diabetes.

Type 2 diabetes, though much rarer in young people and only diagnosed in this age group as recently as 2000, becomes more common with increasing age and is seen far more often in children of South Asian origin. As with adults, obesity is a big risk factor here, alongside ethnic origin.

Overall, diabetes affects boys (52 per cent) slightly more than girls (48 per cent), although Type 2 diabetes is more frequent in girls.

Some general tips

Unlike in adults, diabetes in children will largely be managed by specialist doctors and nurses in hospital paediatric departments, with back-up from their colleagues in general practice. Although they will provide all the education, advice, and guidance needed, you, as a parent or carer, will be responsible for supporting your child in putting these professional words of wisdom into practice. So the following tips might prove useful:

- Spend some time educating yourself about the condition. Knowing the facts will not only put some of the fears that come from the myths about diabetes out of your mind, but will help you manage your child's treatment at home better: from changes in diet and lifestyle, to managing medication and recognizing hypos. Your confidence about the disease will rub off on your children too.

- Be open with any other children in your family about what's going on. Depending on how old they are, their emotions may range widely from fearfulness about what's happening to their brother or sister to jealousy about the attention they're receiving from you – and perhaps a bit of both. Talking to them about diabetes and what it means will help them come to terms with what's happening in the family.

- Make sure you get support from friends and family members and professionals who can be trusted to help you come to terms with your own thoughts, feelings, and struggles about the diagnosis.

- It's not uncommon to feel a sense of guilt when your child develops Type 1 diabetes, but you shouldn't. Nothing you did or didn't do brought it on.

- Be careful not to make the word "diabetic" stand for your child's whole identity by wrapping them in cotton wool all the time. While being mindful of their condition, there is far more to them than that diagnostic label and they need to have a fun childhood as much as anyone else.

School
As your children get older, they will obviously spend a significant part of each day away from you while they are at school. And although many teachers may have taught children with diabetes in the past and know a fair bit about it, not all will have done.

The following tips should keep the worries about their term-time care to a minimum:

- When your child begins primary school and then senior school, ask to meet the key people looking after them, especially their class teacher and form tutor. This will provide an opportunity to see what they do and don't know about diabetes in general and how it will affect your child in particular. This can be backed up with a written care plan so that all those involved in teaching and watching over your child know what's what.

- Make sure the school understands the treatment regime, including when and how insulin has to be given. If you normally give the dose at home, you may need to negotiate how this can be done in the school, particularly if you are at work. If your child injects themselves, you may need to make arrangements for them to do this in private.

- Ensure the school knows how to recognize the symptoms of a hypo and is aware of how to treat it. And gain permission for your child to have any snacks they might need during class – and, as they get older, in exams – in order to prevent them having hypos in the first place.

- Discuss finger-prick blood testing with them so they know when and why this is needed – for example, before PE lessons or playing sports.

- Give the school your contact details in case of difficulties and emergencies and always update them on any changes in these and your child's medication.

The hospital specialist diabetes nurses or school nurses may well be able to help with any training or education the school staff might need.

Children's parties and sleepovers

As is the case when your child's at school, make sure anyone else looking after them, such as a friend's parent at a party or sleepover, knows about their diabetes, details of injections, blood tests, snacking, spotting hypos, and, importantly, your contact details. Written instructions will again be helpful here.

Most importantly of all, as far as your son or daughter will be concerned anyway, tell the other parents that they can eat any of the party food that's served up and that they certainly don't need any special "diabetic food".

Teenage years

Managing your child's diabetes during adolescence is a whole different ball game. As they gain independence and you see less of them, they will have to take more responsibility for their own care – a situation that's made more complicated by the changes in lifestyle that occur at this stage of life. They will still go to parties and have sleepovers, but the parties will have more than fizzy drinks and sausages on sticks to tempt them, and there will often be little sleep during the sleepovers.

The teenage years provide endless opportunities to sample life in all its fullness, from the obvious menu of sex, drugs, and rock and roll, washed down with a generous helping of booze and finished with a cigarette or two, to weekend trips away to summer festivals, gap-year travels to far-flung places, and independent life at university.

As a result, you will need to have some important chats with them to remind them that, although they can still enjoy the riches of life that their friends are experiencing, they have to take extra precautions that their non-diabetic friends don't. And try to make them chats, not sessions of haranguing or lecturing; otherwise, your words are more than likely to fall on deaf and defiant ears.

Special circumstances

The main points to cover with your teenager

- Alcohol makes hypos more likely, so never go out drinking on an empty stomach, always have something to eat before going to bed, and drink plenty of water to avoid dehydration.
- Cannabis can make you so chilled that you forget to take your insulin and can also give you the munchies. Both put you at risk of hyperglycaemia.
- Sex can use up a lot of energy, so beware of hypos. And although it's OK for girls with diabetes to go on the pill, condoms are always a must to ensure safe sex.
- Smoking is bad for everyone but increases the chances of heart disease and stroke to an even greater extent for people with diabetes, so don't make a habit of it.
- When travelling, ensure you have enough needles, syringes, and blood sugar test strips for the entire trip. You should take all of your equipment in your hand luggage. Not only may you need to have your insulin on a long flight, but the temperature in the aircraft's hold may reduce the effectiveness of insulin if it's stored in your main luggage. It's also a good idea to ask your family doctor or specialist for a letter to carry with you, explaining the need to have your medication and needles in the cabin.

Diabetes in older age

Old age, as my more senior patients never cease to remind me, does not come alone. So although most of the advice in this book holds for adults of all ages, it's important to be mindful of some of the ravages of age, which can cause specific problems for people with diabetes and make life that little bit trickier.

Potential problems

I use the word "potential" here because we are all different, and although some age-related physical changes affect some people, they will leave others largely unscathed. Ageing is not, after all, a disease with its own specific set of symptoms.

So, for example, I've been overtaken (embarrassingly easily) by septuagenarians when running half-marathons, but I know other people a decade younger than them whose advanced arthritis forces them to shuffle painfully around the house. And although Charlie Chaplin was famously fathering children well into old age, many men much younger struggle to even raise a smile in the bedroom, let alone anything to help them make babies.

The fact remains that the longer our cells and tissues have been functioning, the more likely they are to experience a bit of wear and tear. And it is this human equivalent of industrial pre-programmed obsolescence that can cause the problems.

Age-related challenges

Here's a quick look at some of the extra challenges that the ageing process can present to people with diabetes.

- *Medication.* As we've seen, managing diabetes and preventing its complications can mean that a daily dose of treatment amounts to swallowing a considerable number of tablets every few hours or so. As we get older, we are more likely to pick up side effects and suffer from drug interactions. So it's important for older people to have regular medication reviews with their doctor or nurse who will be on the look-out for these issues.

- *Memory.* Because of the complicated nature of diabetes treatment and the need to be fully aware of worrying symptoms, such as those of a hypo, any decline in intellectual functioning and memory can cause havoc if it's not identified.

Special circumstances

At the mild to moderate end of the scale, help from carers and other professionals can be arranged to make doses simpler and provide blister packs to avoid confusion about which tablets need to be taken when, and nurses can be enlisted to give insulin injections. At the more severe end of the scale, when someone has full-on dementia, residential or nursing home care may be needed.

- *Meals*. It's as important in old age as it is when we are younger to have a healthy, balanced diet to help control blood sugar in diabetes. Unfortunately, loss of taste and smell, fading eyesight, loneliness and isolation, arthritis, depression, and general lack of interest can all gang up on us as we age, reducing both our desire and physical ability to cook decent meals. Social Services departments can help by arranging provision of various state-run and private meals-on-wheels services, which now suit most tastes and ethnic preferences, and make access to nutritious foods much easier.

- *Sexual activity*. Age should not be a barrier to wanting or being able to have sex. But side effects of multiple medications alongside furring up of arteries can reduce libido (sex drive) and cause erectile dysfunction. These symptoms can often be helped, if not resolved, after a medication review with the doctor and perhaps a prescription for a tablet such as Viagra to sort out any impotence issues.

- *Spotting hypos*. Not only can hypos be more likely to happen in older age because of the combination of a poor diet, multiple medications, and the effects of other illnesses, but they can also be harder to spot. Family and carers need to be aware that headaches, a change in personality and concentration, sleep disturbances, and confusion can all be caused by persistently low blood sugar.

Diabetes and pregnancy

There are two ways in which diabetes and pregnancy can interact: women with pre-existent Type 1 or Type 2 diabetes can become pregnant; and women can develop a specific type of diabetes, called gestational diabetes, when they become pregnant. Both need special monitoring to ensure mother and baby remain well.

Having a baby if you're diabetic

Having diabetes should not deter you from wanting to have a baby. But when you do decide you want to give conception a try, you should first have a chat and a check-up with your family doctor or practice nurse to make sure your diabetes is well enough under control before you start.

They will also need to review your medications to make sure you're not on anything, either for your diabetes or anything else (perhaps blood pressure and/or cholesterol), that may not be safe during pregnancy. If you are, then changes will need to be made, and if it's diabetes pills that are the issue, then you may need to be switched over to insulin until after your baby is born. Once you've had the green light, you will also be prescribed a slightly higher dose of the folic acid that all women take for the first 12 weeks of pregnancy to help prevent neural tube defects such as spina bifida.

Women with diabetes have a higher risk of complications during pregnancy than women who don't, particularly macrosomia (having a big baby) and delivering a baby with hypoglycaemia. So expect more frequent antenatal appointments with your midwife and doctor, a referral to an obstetrician and regular scans.

These professionals will want to make sure you have tight blood sugar control and are not running into problems yourself, such as having frequent hypos. They will also plan for delivery which, depending on how things go, may involve either a caesarean section or your delivery being induced early.

Gestational diabetes

This type of diabetes only happens in pregnancy and is a result of women being unable to produce sufficient insulin to meet the extra demand of growing a baby. It is quite common, affecting around 18 per cent of pregnant women, and, according to the Royal College of Obstetricians and Gynaecologists, is more likely if:

- you've had gestational diabetes before
- you have a close relative with Type 1 or Type 2 diabetes
- your family originated in South Asia, China, the Caribbean, or the Middle East
- your body mass index (BMI) is over 30
- you've had a large baby before (4.5 kg or 10 lbs or more).

If you fall into any of these categories, you will be asked to take a glucose tolerance test (see Chapter 4); if the test suggests that you do have diabetes, then your antenatal care will be as intensive as for a woman with pre-existing diabetes, as discussed above.

Once you've had your baby, the diabetes should settle and you will be able to come off any medication, providing your blood sugar is OK. You will have a follow-up glucose tolerance test 6–8 weeks after delivery to make sure everything is back to normal.

Diabetes and driving

There are a number of medical conditions that the Driver and Vehicle Licensing Agency (DVLA) need to be informed of, and due to the risk of hypos and unconsciousness at the wheel, diabetes is one of them. The risks depend on the type of diabetes you have and the type of vehicle you drive, and although it is very unlikely that you will have to stop driving altogether once diagnosed, the following advice needs to be followed.

Car and motorbike drivers

Unless you are being treated with insulin injections for your diabetes, you ordinarily don't need to inform the DVLA about your diabetes. However, you must notify them if any of the following do subsequently apply to you:

- You suffer more than one episode of severe hypoglycaemia within 12 months.

- You develop difficulty in recognizing the warning symptoms of low blood sugar (hypos).

- You ever suffer severe hypoglycaemia while driving.

- You begin to need treatment with insulin.

- You need laser treatment to both eyes or in the remaining eye if you have sight in one eye only.

- You have problems with vision in both eyes or in the remaining eye if you only have sight in one eye.

- You develop any problems with your circulation or sensation in your legs or feet that make it necessary for you to drive only certain types of vehicle – for example, automatic vehicles or vehicles with a hand-operated accelerator or brake.

Buses and lorries

Driving bigger vehicles obviously carries bigger risks, so restrictions are tighter. There is a three-stage application process which involves completing an application form, filling in a specialist questionnaire, and having a medical examination by a diabetes specialist.

In order to be successful, your application must tick the following boxes:

- You have had no hypoglycaemic event requiring the help of another person in the last 12 months.

- You must have full awareness of the symptoms of hypoglycaemia.

- You must be able to show an understanding of the risks of hypoglycaemia.

- You must check your blood sugar/glucose levels at least twice daily, even on non-driving days, and within two hours of the start of the first journey and every two hours while driving. This must be done using a blood sugar/glucose meter with a memory function to measure and record blood glucose levels.

- You must keep a fast-acting carbohydrate within reach when driving.

- You must attend an examination every 12 months with an independent consultant specializing in the treatment of diabetes.

- You must have at least three months of continuous blood sugar/glucose readings available on the memory of your blood sugar/glucose meter(s) for the consultant to inspect. These readings must have been taken while being treated with insulin.

- You must have no other debarring medical condition.

- You must sign an agreement stating that you will comply with the directions of doctors treating your diabetes and that you will report immediately any significant changes.

For more information about driving and diabetes, please refer to the DVLA website: www.gov.uk/diabetes-driving.

Mythbuster

Diabetes stops you playing sports.

No, it doesn't. In fact, many people with diabetes have been successful athletes – Olympic rowing champion Sir Steve Redgrave is a great example. It's a good idea to discuss blood sugar management with your doctor or nurse before you start, but the condition should not stop you taking part.

Appendix 1: Blood sugar biology

Here is a quick run-through of what should happen to our body's levels of blood sugar in the few hours after we've eaten something. We will begin by looking at what glucose is and then follow the journey of a molecule of this sugar that's contained in a chocolate muffin from first tasty mouthful to metabolism into an energy source for the body's cells. (Don't worry, we won't follow the waste bits all the way out!)

Glucose

Every organism alive, from the simplest bacteria to the most complex mammal, uses the sugar molecule glucose as one of its main sources of fuel to produce the internal energy that's needed to allow all of life's most basic functions to continue. So whether you are a squid, a squirrel, or a Scandinavian, it is as essential to your continued life on this planet as oxygen.

Glucose is found in a wide range of natural foods, particularly fruit, nuts, vegetables, and honey. And it's found, often in huge quantities, in manufactured foods such as cakes, doughnuts, fizzy drinks, fruit juice, and, of course, sweets and chocolate bars. It's also the building block of much bigger carbohydrate molecules such as the starch found naturally in rice, potatoes, pasta, bread, and chocolate muffins.

To get from its packet on the supermarket shelf into your muscles or brain cells, our muffin first has to go through the process of digestion, so that its glucose can be released.

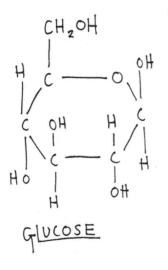

C = CARBON
H = HYDROGEN
O = OXYGEN

The molecular structure of glucose

Digestion

Digestion begins with the very first mouthful as the muffin is broken into smaller pieces as we bite into and then chew it. Our saliva contains the chemical enzyme called amylase and this starts to break large carbohydrate molecules, such as starch, into their smaller constituent sugar molecules, before they even leave the mouth.

Once swallowed, the mushed-up muffin is squeezed down the oesophagus (gullet) with the help of muscle contractions known as peristalsis until it reaches the stomach. Here, the larger molecules are broken up further by the action of hydrochloric acid before being sloshed into the next part of the guts, the small intestines, where the majority of their digestion takes place.

It's here that they are bombarded by yet more enzymes, which chemically break them up into their smallest constituents, including glucose. This can then be absorbed through the walls of the bowel and pass from these into the surrounding blood vessels.

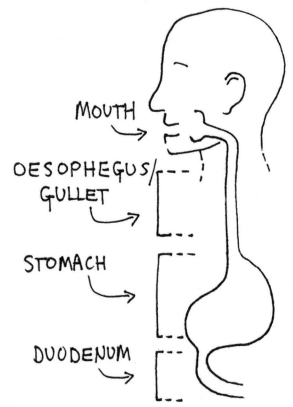

MOUTH

OESOPHEGUS/ GULLET

STOMACH

DUODENUM

The digestive tract

Blood sugar control

Once in the blood, glucose is then available as fuel for all of the cells around the body, but, most importantly, for those in the brain and nervous system which rely almost exclusively on glucose to power them (other cells can make use of fats). However, as with so many things in life, you can have too much (as well as too little) of a good thing, and too much glucose being pumped around in the blood can cause problems, as we see in diabetes. So there are two hormones, both produced in the pancreas gland, whose job it is to try to keep the level stable: insulin and glucagon.

Insulin

Insulin has the starring role in our story about diabetes. It is produced in the pancreas in the wonderfully named Islets of Langerhans, which sound more like geographical features on a distant planet in a *Star Wars* film than clusters of cells inside the human body.

Once manufactured in the beta cells within the Islets, insulin is ready to be released into the bloodstream when levels of sugar rise, soon after a full-on meal or after snacking on a muffin. There are receptors to insulin in the walls of cells in both the liver and our muscles, and when insulin attaches to them (rather like a plug fitting into a socket) a string of chemical reactions is set in motion inside these cells which trigger the following processes:

- Glucose is absorbed into the cells from the bloodstream.

- Once inside, this glucose is converted into another chemical called glycogen, so that it can be stored.

- The reverse process of existing glycogen being turned back into glucose is stopped.

The end result is that the blood level of glucose goes down.

Glucagon

This hormone is also made in the Islets of Langerhans, but this time in alpha cells. Its job is the opposite to that of insulin and so it is released into the bloodstream when sugar levels are low. There are glucagon receptors on liver cell walls (which are obviously quite crowded places!), and when glucagon molecules fix to them, the following chemical reactions occur:

- Glycogen stores are converted into glucose.
- Glucose is made from amino acids in the cell.
- Fat cells are broken down so that their constituents can also be used for energy.

The end result here is a rise in blood glucose.

So whether you are munching on a muffin or between meals, these two hormones will make sure you still have the right amount of glucose in your blood to give you the energy you need to get on with your day. It's a different story, of course, if you have diabetes, because you either have too little insulin, insensitive receptors, or both, and so your blood glucose levels are out of control.

Appendix 2: Useful resources

The list below, though not exhaustive, includes organizations whose websites are useful sources of advice and guidance about all aspects of diabetes care and management. Some are provided by charities, and others are government-run, but all contain the latest information to help you look after your diabetes and, most importantly, yourself. Given that the worldwide web is just that – worldwide – you can dip in to any of these sites wherever you are from and make the most of the help they have to offer.

United Kingdom
www.diabetes.org.uk
Diabetes UK, Britain's largest diabetes charity, provides information and advice about all aspects of Type 1 and Type 2 diabetes, helps to raise public awareness of the condition and supports research.

www.diabetes.co.uk
This website, branded "the global diabetes community", covers everything from details of drug treatments for diabetes to recipe ideas for a healthy diet.

www.nhs.uk
The UK's National Health Service website features a wealth of information about diabetes alongside pages on any other medical condition you can think of.

www.patient.info
Another site with information about all medical conditions but with detailed sections on all aspects of diabetes.

Australia
www.diabetesaustralia.com.au
This national diabetes charity raises funds to invest in research, health services, provision of self-management products and services, and public awareness programmes. Its website is a rich source of information.

www.healthdirect.gov.au
This website is a hub for health information on all conditions, including diabetes. Its content is evidence-based and it provides useful links to partner websites.

Canada
www.diabetes.ca
The mission of the Canadian Diabetes Association is to lead the fight against diabetes by helping those affected by the disease to live healthy lives, preventing the onset and consequences of diabetes, and discovering a cure. The site has information about all aspects of the condition from childhood to old age.

 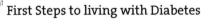

New Zealand
www.diabetes.org.nz
Diabetes New Zealand is the national charity of New Zealand which aims to represent and support people diagnosed with the condition. The website has details on all aspects of diabetes from diagnosis to advice on leading a healthy lifestyle.

United States
www.diabetes.org
The American Diabetes Association is one of the largest organizations of its kind in the world and its website is a great resource for anyone with diabetes.

Acknowledgments

I'd like to thank the editorial team at Lion Hudson for their wonderful support in putting this book together, with particular thanks going to Alison Hull, who as commissioning editor has been an encouragement to me since trying me out with my first *First Steps* book. Thanks, Ali, for this opportunity to keep writing and for all the advice and fine-tuning along the way.

Thanks also to my son Sam, who has again provided the lovely illustrations for this book, squeezing me in while trying to concentrate on his own, more important, art projects for his art A level.